Acknowledgments

❧

I would like to thank the Lord, who is the instrument of peace. Not only do I feel His presence in my life, but He speaks to me through my Music and Poetry.

I would also like to extend my deep appreciation to my wonderful husband Dick, to whom a lot of my poetry is about and the love we share.

To my family – without them I would not be here.

And an extra special thanks to my true friends – those who love me and accept me for who I am.

All of everyone's encouragement and support is a blessing.

Patty

Go quietly –
Like soft rose pedals
Setting on an open stream
Rushing water –
Across standing rocks
Visions of a land of paradise
Sun striking down –
Upon the earths greenest ground –
And all of God's creatures are standing around
Go quietly – in peace –
Let the silence embrace your soul

Days

Yesterday
you loved me

Today
you loved me more

Tomorrow
you are forever

Anger

Inside
clusters of anger
like building blocks
stacking one by one

No color to each piece
dullness –
like looking through glass –
with no reflection

Never ending, but
cutting through
leaving deep scars
that never fade

As the sun rises every morning –
A new day is just beginning
When the sun sets in the evening –
A star appears
For God is near you

∞

Music is the gift of your soul

Understanding one's inner feelings

Solos that lift your spirit

Inside each musician is a

Concert

Music

Lost in a rainbow –
entwined in a circle of colors
Going on forever through
the clouds and heavens
Feeling like a part
of the universe
and never stopping
for a rest
Holding on to
a dream that
lasts forever and
feeling no pain –
except for the
past – fearing you
will never come back

a day has gone by
like the wind
blowing freely –
and I could
feel you there
behind my footsteps
Wanting you
touching you
knowing you
will follow me
forever
for I am
not home yet
but my journey
is not long
away
and my love
for you is
closer than the morning

In loving memory of my Grandmother Rose Astuno

Remembering Christmas Eve

It seems like only yesterday
Christmas Eve was in the air
Remembering the little things
that made us feel at home

The smell of the fish –
the steam on the windows –
Rushing with no time to spare

To all be together
this one time of year
where love and laughter
filled the living room air

→

The excitement of us children
waiting for that magic moment
of opening presents one by one

Torn boxes everywhere
with paper covering Grandmothers floor
while Grandpa sat in his
big green chair, with a little
smile lasting only a while

And mother and father making sure
we had eaten before we had
cookies and pie

All in six hours we managed
to see the happiest of Christmases
that memories did bring

Alone –
four walls closing you in
No sound
No meaning
No love
It's cruel out there
Time – there
is no time
Time is like a wheel
that turns from
day to day
Never stopping
Just turning –
but yet it takes you
with it
You have no choice
No power
to stop time
it just lingers on

In memory of the crew of the Space Shuttle Challenger

OUR HEROES

They wanted to touch the stars –
to feel like children of the moon

They wanted to soar like the eagles –
to be proud of the universe

They wanted to study the future and
share it with the world

They wanted to hold onto a dream –
a dream that would last a lifetime

But instead they became part of the sky
They became stars that will shine forever

In the
corner of
my room
strung within
my thoughts
Scratches lie
deeply engraved
from the victories
of each match –
my tennis racket

Dew on morning grass
frost upon the window
last night's dream
out of mind
a new day
reborn

❧

Time you
will find
an answer
Time you
will find
yourself

Betrayal

Betrayal
Comes like
A fire
Striking with
No warning –
Flames burn
My heart
Tearing every
Vessel apart –
No reason –
No shame –
A war with no ending –
Will the peace
Ever find
Me

Come to
me
softly
let your
eyes set
upon me
like a star
in the sky
on an
endless night
Let your
kiss be
gentle like
a flower
growing wild –
let us be
of one
forever

Dreams Above

High above are the
      dreams I love
Up above is the
      sky God holds
Far away is
      where I pray –
for my dreams will
come true someday

                   ॐ

Love is . . .
      an endless rainbow only we travel

Only the days
of learning what
life is about
is the time
your journey begins
Life brings many
challenges and
times you can
not change –
Believe in where
your heart leads
and you will
find that
today is not
forever, but
tomorrow is only
minutes away

Flight

soft clouds
pending
wingless birds –
a rage of
glacier clouds
touching
dead of night
overshadows of
terror
a long struggling
flight –
morning light

In this empty room
I can see your face
looking straight out at me
But you are so very
far away –
and I long for each
hour of the day
to pass by faster
than a shooting star
so you can be here
to dry up my tears

Friend

If a friend
is worth searching for
be on your journey

Glowing
are your eyes
Set upon
the sunrise
warming
my heart –
reaching for love
I touch you
In moments
we fade together into
the sunset

༄

Love is a warm understanding
Open for everyone
Very Strong
Endless
Love

GOD

Give me the strength
to find who I am

Show me the path
that has all the answers

Take away the fear
and replace it with courage

Give me the love
so I can give it to others

Find me a friend
who will give me their heart

Help me find patience
and destroy all hatred

and in return I will
believe and follow you forever

In loving memory of our Grandmother, Helen Acierno
... Roxanne, Patty & Denise

In my little four-room house,
I raised my family with tender love and understanding
Though times were tough, and money low,
I always prayed God would see us through

I'll always remember the smell of my kitchen –
with food always cooking for all who came by
Those were the memories – oh, how they flew by

And not to forget my husband, my dear,
who spent his whole life in his small, treasured barn
The cooing of pigeons would fill up the air, and
leave you with feelings that God must be there

My garden of flowers engulfed our small yard
The vision of roses brought light to my life

As I sat on my porch at the end of the day,
I always found time for that last bit of yarn –
to knit something special to send all your way

I enjoyed special occasions
I saw laughter and tears
God granted me my sight to see my grandchildren,
great grandchildren, and even great-great grandchildren
Five generations all through the years

I've held you and rocked you,
and gave you all the love in my heart
And now, I must leave you

My Theresa, my Marie, my Snookie, my Violet —
Be happy for me, for you cannot imagine
what I am feeling right now
I was met by your Daddy, and my sweet little Georgie
The angels were singing, the clouds opened wide,
and suddenly I realized my pain was all gone

It wasn't a house, or money, or fame
that made me the person that I became
I lived such a long life, and I need to go home
Remember — I love you, and you are never alone

God Bless Each and Every One of You

I'm sorry
I missed you today –
sometimes there are
moments we forget
who we are
or the value of
what a friend
really is –
next time I'll
remind myself
to take the
time to say hello
or at least
a warm smile

Friendship

Your friendship
    no keys
    no locks
Just an ever open door

Haiku

a new flower growing wild
opens to the colors of a rainbow
soon it will die

I love you

I love you today
    I love you tomorrow
        I love you forever

∾

I found heaven
I found life
I found meaning
When I met you –
I found everything

I touch
your hand
it gives warmth

I touch
your eyes
they brighten my life

I touch your heart –
Giving streams of happiness
I touch your love
you give so easily

I touch you
as we grow closer
you touch me
in such beautiful ways
I am a part of you

My life is a house of mirrors
getting lost in a maze
that never seems to quit

Life is a roller coaster ride
going up and down all the time
turning everything upside down

Life is playing games
Friends go by just like the wind
No matter how hard you try
you never seem to win

I will always be with you
in your heart and mind
To remind you to always
be patient and kind

To live each day for
all that it is worth and
wish for tomorrow,
but never in sorrow

I will always be with you
the rest of your lives, giving,
and sharing what life is about

For I will follow you
each and every day, and
I pray that your love
will always remain

Life

Empty hopes and shattered dreams
haunt me day by day –

I don't know what it really is
that makes me feel this way –

All are a part of memories –
some I wish I could leave behind

Rushing days and restless nights
I don't know what is wrong or right –

A hollow heart
an empty mind
A bundle of muscles entwined –

I really wish there
was something out there –

Something for me to find

Friends are for keeps
Remembering fun times
Is someone to turn to
Endless in many ways
Never breaking up
Depending on each other
Sharing your secrets
Helping you cope with problems
Is someone you can trust
Pleasing one another

Friendship

In the
days I find
your smiles and
dreams for tomorrow –
I search for
your love –
like a song
sometimes the
notes will fade
into a sea
of apathy
drowning us forever

Inside
shoving – like a
mean bluster
of torture
destroyed – offended
not clear – just hurting
like forcible wind –
swirling through
cries let out
a stream of emotions

Through all the years
of loving you –
You've taught me
more than words can say

Through good times
and bad times –
We have faced the
world side by side

Through every intimate moment
Each of our hearts
become as one –
Like a dove gliding
into the morning sun

Whenever I am lost
You wash away my tears
and shine a light
that sets me free –
I love you more than anything

Lost
in your love –
like tattered webs
there is no escape
so hopelessly –
I search
for your
touch –
your love that you promise
and just
as we are
drawn together
the string
that attaches
us is
broken

Life

Life is not
an easy road
It changes directions
but yet we are
fools and take it
for granted
Never a question to
where we are going
too proud –
We search on our own
looking for answers –
the world is full
of deafness
people hear only themselves
and are lost forever –
searching

I have been
Called home
To this everlasting light
And though you cannot
See me
Or touch me –
Please know that
I am near you
I know your heart
Is broken –
Your tears are
Surely flowing
But never
Will I leave you
Your memories
Continue to
Relieve me

Search

I search
long and far
forever
for you –
but only see
a vision too
far to reach
too fragile to
touch
too easy to break
I search

Life is a mystery
Too complex to us all
The world is far
from perfect
and answers seem unresolved

There is anger
all around us
with patience
hard to find
until a heart is broken
then someone
comes around

But every day goes by us
some up and others down
and forever we are searching
for nothing to be found

My dream

Like a dream
you came
so free –
like beauty touching
my soul but
no pain
Here you'll stay
forever growing
so easily –
Like a dream

Life is like a puzzle
piece by piece you
discover what the world
is made of and what
direction you should follow

Many time the pieces
don't fit or match
and the frustration
makes you feel like crumbling

Hold on to yourself
for life has a million
pieces to a puzzle
and it takes more than
one day to complete –

It takes a lifetime

I have lived a long and privileged life –
In a world of love and paradise
But the time has come when I must leave –
And in your heart is where I'll be
Saint Francis has taken me to another place
Where no one else can see
A place where sunshine warms my back –
As I lay in this heavenly grass green
Just call my name, and I will be your vision
For I have been set free

I thought I knew
the answer to
most of life's questions –
but little did
I know there is
a giant barricade
blocking most of
the dreams important
to us all –

Reality is just
around the corner
lurking like a
little black crow
that never stops
following every step you take –
and when you
take that
big chance you
have always waited for –
you find yourself
back at the beginning

Lord

You are my life –
Every breath that I take

As the sun shines through
my window pane
you bring light to each
and every day

As long as the rivers flow –
As long as the flowers bloom –
You are in my heart
Your love will never part

When I am afraid and
feel alone and astray –
I just call out your name
and you show me the way

Love is a feeling
Love is a song
Love is so special
When you are around

Love is two people
Just you and me
What makes it so
special is what
I found in you

It seems I'm holding
the whole world
on my shoulders –
Lord knows why
I just don't
let it go
Forgive me if
I can't turn away
Here I stand –
I'm just a victim
I can hear you
in the darkness
of the night
telling me
Give it one
more chance –
Trust in me
and I will
bring you home
and free your
broken heart

Love takes time
It takes feeling
It takes one's heart
To love another

Love takes pride
It takes confidence
It takes courage to
Continue to love equally

Love takes patience
It takes caring
It takes forgiving when
One is wrong

But most of all –
Love takes trust
It takes knowing whenever
You are apart
That your love is forever

If a mountain be too steep to climb
the wind has touched your back
for a person can conquer anything
if they follow the right track

If there be a time of loneliness
where the sun has hardly shined
look into the blue-gray skies
for a friend is what you'll find

If the road seems like it goes forever
in the direction that you chose —
let a friend travel with you
for you have nothing to lose

When you sit all alone sometimes
and there is nothing there to do —
just remember there is a true friend
thinking of you too

My World

When I am alone
    each day

I walk along this
    world so gray

Until I reach the end of day
that's why my world
is so far away

In a slow motion
daze – you came
into my life –
like being born
once again – we
grew closer
leaving behind the seeds
we grew by

On an ordinary day,
With not a worry or nothing to fear –
My life was taken abruptly from me
The panic, the screaming,
The blood and the tears –
Then silence, as I lie in a room
With my peers
The mountains were hidden
By a mysterious cloud –
Then I knew that my Savior
Had come to take me
Have courage for all the
Great sorrows of life –
Go to sleep in peace and
Always remember me

My Friend

As time goes by our
friendship has gone

It seems I can't understand
why we can't go on

My tears wet my cheek
as I think of the times
I wish we could keep

I wonder and wonder
if there is someone to keep

Well, all those times are gone
and there is nothing left beyond

If I could be a rainbow –
I'd shine on you when
you feel blue

If I could be a sparrow –
I'd fly your distance
when you tire

If I could be a mountain –
I'd stand up tall
when you feel small

For I can be most anything
if you believe in me

I'm free now —
But always beside you —

When the wind picks up
Please know it is me

When the sunrise comes
Over the mountain tops —
Remember I am looking
At thee

When the rain pours down
And the skies are gray —
Do not be sad
For God makes these days

When the snow falls on
Your window pane —
Think of me as your angel
Coming to stay

For I will always be a vision
In everything you see -
And remain near you in all
Your times of need

My life
is like
a picture
taken from
the past –
Remembering
that certain
moment and
expression –
Drifting into
the future
a step
at a time –
recalling every
moment that
you left behind
New pictures
New dreams
all are a part of
a painted picture –
framed within your mind

I have lived a long
And wonderous Life –
Longer than most dogs
Could ever hope for –
I was a champion,
With many ribbons to show –
But it was my kind soul that
Everyone got to know –
I am free now,
I am in a better place –
Saint Francis is now
Looking over me

Nervousness

On the
tennis courts
I met nervousness
He tugged at my racket –
my hands
couldn't hold on
"Don't hit it back"
"Give them the shot"
he said
He's hot as can be –
Made me sweat
like a dog
"You'll never win"
"Can't you feel the wind?"
"It will sweep you
right of your feet," he said
He stayed
with me through
the entire match –
I lost

Seems only yesterday
life began for me –
leaving the past
looking toward the future
a step at a time
tears along the way
fighting to know the answers
wondering if
you'll survive
so many friends
smiles, tears and laughter
Sunny days
rainy nights
unforgotten dreams
so much
to experience
so much to let go
prayers to start again
time to grow
but only you
will know

On this Dark
And sober night
Red-hot rage
Was in the air –
The beast within –
Took innocent people –
Such panic and fear –
Tiny screams
And shattered silence
No one knew their
Life would end
Angel whispered –
Take my hand – step out
Of the darkness
And into the light

Friends

A friend is nothing
but a memory
like a shadow
that is never seen
And then you wake up
and see that
friendship is all
but a dream

You were my
Soul mate
My Velcro boy –
Oh how I miss
Your warmth
Your smell –
I'm sorry you were taken
With no chance to survive
And we could not
Save you –
Your innocence lives on
Saint Francis
Has you in
His loving arms
Forever more
My little boy
My friend

My life is worth
More than anything
And I will become
The best of everything

God will be with me every day –
For I know I am better off this way

࿋

Sometimes friends
are like the yellow pages
You have to look them up
before you really know who they are

On the edge of
reality lies a road
with many answers –

If you could see
tomorrow only a
vision would be
waiting there

Today is an
illusion drifting
hour by hour

No one knows the future
it waits for you –
haunting you in
your dreams

Once In A Lifetime

Once in a lifetime
Someone special
comes around –
and touches your heart
In the deepest ways –

Someone who cares
Someone who makes
you feel each
day worthwhile –

Once in a lifetime
Someone stands near you –
Shows you the way
makes every step
a rainbow

Once in a lifetime
Someone finds a person like you
and their once in a
lifetime's become every day

<u>Only Yesterday</u>

Only yesterday
I walked along a vacant
road searching for an answer

Only yesterday
I held onto a dream
that haunts me day by day

Only yesterday
I hurt the one I love
and in turn destroyed
my own heart

Only yesterday
I found I was
lost and turned
back around to
come back home again

Open the door
and let me in
to all good things that
this world brings

Give me a chance
to stay for a while
at least for as
long as a smile or two

Help me find courage
and strength from within
to give to others
the talents I bring

Just open the door
and you will see
that I bring you
peace from deep within

We are innocent children
So why are we the ones to die –
You once heard our laughter
We walked down our little school halls

The sound of loud explosions
The glass is everywhere –
I'm lying here in darkness
Tears of blood run down my face

How could this have happened?
I'm not ready to be free
I heard a voice from heaven –
It's ok – Just follow me

<u>Pictures</u>

Torn pictures
of the past
like shattered kaleidoscopes
never to be focused
Each microscopic piece
fades like shadows
no memories –
like a puzzle
with missing pieces
gone – forever
pictures

My life is
like a pendulum
swaying from one
corner to the next
Answers unspoken
like a dream
I drift away
into a passage
of time –
Never seeing what
lies ahead of me
and slowly I
come to the end
of a journey
that never existed
but time is
still ticking away

Shadows
of two
in love
reaching out
Souls
reflecting across
water
like a sea
filled with
dreams and
promises to
be born

Perhaps Death

Alone one day
I walked along this vacant trail
to find there was no
end of day –
terrified – I can't turn back –
I had found that
death is a little black bird
that sits perched ahead of my
trails
waiting – to

Be Near Me

Be Near me
When the light is low –
For I am not afraid –
The angels
Are surrounding me –
The music
Like a choir –
I feel you in my presence
But it is time
For me to go
I know that you are weeping
But the Lord
Will take me home

In the beginning
I loved you for a very long time
Thinking it would last forever

Like a child
You clinged to me –
For you felt safe
But never gave me
Much of anything

Now you wander
Away from me –
With no guilt, no reason, nor shame
It is all but just a bad dream

I want to know why
You have become this person inside –
This horribly dreadful thing

Search
long
Search
far
Follow
your shadow
closely
You are
Not alone –
only driven
to the
point of
madness
Hold on –

Searching

Heaven knows
You are going to
search everywhere you go –
Find me where
I am hiding –
Call me and I
will come to you
I will walk my
longest mile and
face my hardest trial
and when it hurts
too much to cry –
I will let my sprit fly

There is a small child –
the child within us
It cries out
in everything
that you do –
It follows you closely
controlling every move
that you make
You cannot survive
without it –
It's like a heart that
keeps beating –
Never slowing you down
and forever driving you
into a dream that's
gone mad –
and just when you
think you are at the
end of this nightmare –
you find yourself
at the beginning

Mom Has Gone to Heaven
No More Suffering,
No More Pain –
She Went to be with Jesus
As She Met Him at His Gate

She Was Surrounded by Her Roses
Every Color at Her Feet –
As She Walked Forward
Her Loved Ones Were There
For Her to Meet

I Know You May Be Crying
You Will Miss Me
For I Am Gone –
But There Is No Greater Place
I Have Ever Found

Solo

I look
into myself
and give to
others
the gift of
my soul
I sometimes pause
to think a while
what I want to
offer
Then with no
time – just
inner feeling
I play for them
so freely

Teardrops and Rain

On a dull and
rainy day
I walked along the road
and prayed
As the rain came pouring down –
a tear hit my cheek as
I began to weep
Confused as I was
I walked on until dawn –
till the rain had stopped
pouring down

Without Your Love

The world would not revolve
without your love

The sun just wouldn't shine
without your love

The wind would not be free
without your love

I just wouldn't be me
without your love

- I Love You -

Memory

Within my thoughts
a memory
left
pasted in my
mind
a childhood
past
remembrances alone
times I left
searching –
of meaning – enough
perhaps only a place
across mountains
clear visions – open
but cold
like tattered webs
no escape
in my mind
pasted

Your Friendship

Within
your friendship
answers to questions –
life's given feelings
– understanding –

Growing to know you
special times will
never fade
– memories –

Time I find
– meaning –

Your Friendship

The Game

Torn between two worlds –
like a game
for two players
never getting ahead
but losing every time
Trapped within a time
where no answers exist –
    No objects
    No logic
And then as you get
to the end of the game –
you feel like your
at the beginning

Why is this
World full of violence?
Anger filling
Hearts and Souls
Like the wind –
You know it's there –
Howling deep within
Cries of a broken heart –
As smoke bursts into
The once blue sky

As I stare at you –
I look into a mirror
A faint reflection
comes over me
for even though
we look different –
we share the same
world

touch me
for I will become a shining star
kiss me
for I will become an open
stream
hold me
for I will melt inside of you
love me
for I will never stop

The Mountains

Across the shadows of
the mountains
A doe in the rain –
the scent of flowers fill the air
The pine is fresh –
The rabbits play –
for it is God's day

The Kite

In
the
air
green
and
red
climb
the
stairs
torn
white
bows
kite

You

You
touch my life
You
touch the warmth of my eyes
You
touch the happiness of my smile
for You
are the guide to all life's desires

The road
has several pathways
leading to the
destinations you desire
some are long and
take a lifetime
Others are short
and have no values
Some roads are bumpy
and hard to follow
Some are icy and
dangerous to travel
But there is only one road
that will never fool you –
one road that is forever beautiful
one road that will never end

Your Love

Your love is beautiful
Your love is kind
Your love is the best
anyone can find

જ

On the top of a mountain
what is there to hear
but a thousand echoes?

Together –
No clouds will ever
surround us –
No river will ever
drown us –

We are forever

Through Passages of Time

Through passages of time
Like a book you filled these pages

On the first page –
Kindness through your words

On the second page –
Understanding in your heart

On the third page –
Love that touched my soul

On the fourth page –
Trust – Stronger than the two of us

On the fifth page –
Happiness in peacock blue colors

On the sixth page –
Strength to build us stronger

On the seventh page –
Desire holding on to what we built

And on the final page –
Your inner beauty

Through Passages of Time

Time Wasted

Today is the beginning
of all yesterdays
Promises no one knows –
for the future
holds a mystery to us all

Every minute ticks away
like a pulse of one's heart
being torn away –
leaving nothing but time
to run out

Precious moments lost –
forgetting what life holds the most
All in a day
Nothing but time wasted

Near my door
He looked at me
Follow me he said –
It is time to say goodbye
To this world you will
Leave behind
I know you will
Have eternal life
No crying
Or no pain –
And someday be reunited
With those who call your name

You & Me

for
we are like
a book –
each page a
happy ending

Today I saw
the shadow of springtime
against my shoulders
in the brightness of day

Finding my weakness
then blinding me by
it's power –

Taking me down to
the end of the universe
to only find out
that I was lost –
but the sun will
soon find me

Why

Why does it always rain
when you want the sun
to shine?

Why do flowers bloom
when you know they are going to
die?

Why do people love –
while others hate?

Tell me why
there is such a word
that we create?

Together

together we
   laugh and smile
together we
   give and share
together we
   know and feel
love

Wonder

I had a feeling
deep inside
Every person and
heart knows –
It cries out of
every corner
at the thing we call life
It is an emotion that
can't be born
or destroyed
It's just there
forever

What is friendship –
will I never know?
Friends will come
others will go
Leaving emptiness
and nothing but pain

The times I treasured
are lost forever
For now I am
nothing but a stranger

An empty heart
Who plays the part?
Do I go back
to the very start?

Trapped

a time
to wander
away
shades of darkness
cling before me
fear
echo's screeching
in the night
my mind
flashes back to
emotions of
ocean breezes
brushing forward – but
frozen
feeling so
empty – cold – and
dark
trapped

In Memory of Those Lives Lost on Flight 17 Over the Ukraine

It all came suddenly
Without a single warning –
Life stolen by a manmade force–
Then everyone was gone
A sweet young girl with tender eyes –
A man of age and wisdom –
A baby in its mothers arms –
Now God's Angel child
Gazing at the smoky clouds –
In the burning sky –
Many hearts ache with pain and sorrow –
For they never said goodbye

Visions

Looking through the
mirrors of life –
I see visions
of yesterday –
Times where I can't
remember who I am
or where I began –
Like illusions in
a dream – Blurring
the place in time
where it all started –
Finding no end
to this long and
everlasting journey –
trapped within
a maze forever –
finding there is
no end

When Love Is Set Free

When love is set free
One learns from the heart
to be on a journey
but never apart –
to learn from each other
the gift of one's self
and never stop loving
from the moment you've met

When love is set free
time draws you closer
to moments of pleasure
of loving each other
and when time comes
to know that your
love has real meaning –
love is together forever

Who am I?

Sometimes I don't know who I am
    or how I feel
    or how I think
Sometimes I feel like shattered
glass, and I can't pick up the pieces
Sometimes I can't really tell
    where I'm going or
    where I'm really leading to
Sometimes I feel I'm
    in a tattered web
    that has no end
and many times when I'm
walking by, I often wonder
who am I?

I love you for
all the wonderful things
you are to me

You are the best friend
anyone could possibly be

You bring joy to my life
and take away all pain

I'll never be lost –
as long as you are near
For I know
as long as we're together

the world is a
better place to be

I Sit Here

I sit here in darkness
I feel so alone –
I know you will
Never come back
To your home
The clock keeps on ticking
The hours go by
My heart cries and beats
As the days linger on –
The winter upon us
Cold wind at your feet
The cries of the wild
Whom we hope not to meet
Every season will come –
As the trees tell us so –
But the emptiness
Will always remain
In my soul

Alone

Alone – I find myself
In a waking dream
A prisoner of my heart
Inside I sleep –
I keep searching
But know you are gone
Taken from my soul –
Like an unfinished song –
Feels like forever
I have been in this state
Closing my eyes
Laden with tears
In darkness I wait

A Woman of Strength

A woman of strength
Has courage within
To face her tomorrows
And never fall down
Her heart may be heavy
Her tears very steady
The shortest days end
And life always begins

Pain

The painfulness of
accomplishment –
when others do
not see it –
Lost in their own
little worlds
not caring what you feel
A tear to them
means nothing
They are sheltered in a shell
So hard that no one
reaches them
Until the shell
Is broken

Without warning

Without warning
You stabbed me
With a dagger
Called betrayal —
No emotions
No remorse
Jealous minds
Are seldom kind
Creating lies —
You are all
On the other side —
But some day will come
To meet your fate —
Will you be
Unchained from your
Emptiness?

Each day he lived
His pain consumed
But why
He chose to
Lose control –
The innocence of people –
The breath of life
Taken too soon –
In a minute's time
Flashes of light
Sounds of fright
And then God whispered –
Come with me

Winter

Winter upon us
The cold at our feet –
The sun set is hiding –
Every road that you meet
The silence around you
Is a moment in time –
Till tomorrow comes
As you sleep

Little girl

Who is this little girl
Who cries inside of me –
Was once a little baby –
Had reason to believe
Just wanted to be accepted –
In a world that paves the way

Who is this little girl
Who was told she
Was nothing but a fool –
Just looking for an answer
For I just don't understand

Who is this little girl
With scars that are so deep and
Etched within my heart –
Perhaps it's just a memory –
But haunts me everyday

Birds

Bluebird sitting in the tree
Your colors like the sky
Tender voice of happiness
As you sing a happy song

Raven soaring in the sky –
Above the mountains oh so high
My heart is held hostage
As you fly by

Tiny brown sparrow –
Beside my window pane
Abandoned by her mother
Protected from the rain

Morning doves calling –
Souls merge into one
Life's journey is surrendered
God will take us all home

Black Crow
On the whitest snow
Are you lost
Or in despair

Your feathered wings
Beneath the green
On where you stand
Upon this land

The edge of night
From your long flight
In the darkness
There is no light

Cold

The cold wind is blowing
The snow is falling
The last of the leaves have hit the ground
My heart is crying
Like a wingless bird dying maybe tomorrow
My senses will find me

∂

Twinges of sadness
Melting in my soul
Like a scar
It's a magnet
For everyone
I've known
I can taste the sweet
Bitter flavor of pain –
From being broken deep inside

Your Life was a blessing

Your Memory a treasure –

They will linger –

In my heart forever

The laughter –

The tears –

The times you were near –

The music we shared

We knew God was there

A true champion you were

You fought hard

Till the end

Don't Settle

Don't settle for nothing less
For you deserve the best
Aim a little higher
You can do anything you desire
Lost behind was a path
Memories change
Feelings fade
Just keep traveling
and you'll find happiness
It is a state of mind

Betrayal

I spent many years –
Gave you my heart
My trust in
What I thought
Was true friendship
Feeling safe
Gave it my all –
To find out you
You betrayed it all
Sinful lies –
Putting a knife
In my heart
Crying raindrops –
A devil
In disguise

Endless dreams –
A restless night
Lost in a world –
Unable to fight –
Helpless – Lost –
Feeling blind
With no sight –
A warped journey
Ending with no
Paradise
And in the morning
When the sun
Should rise –
A cloud of
Darkness across
The sky

The Breast Cancer Patient

As you go through this unpredictable journey
Let me not walk behind you
Nor in front of you –
But beside you
For each step we take together
Hand in hand
Will give us
Hope, strength and courage
Some days we may stumble –
Other days we may fall –
But there is nothing that will keep us
From standing tall –
And when we get to the road to recovery
It will seem like each day
Is now a beginning

I guess I was too clingy
So, I tried to give you space
But you only threw it
Right back into my face
I'll give you time alone
As you simply fade away
Another month has come
And you are still so far away
Your always in my heart
I thought we had that friendship from
the start
My tears are surely flowing
But doubt you will ever know

Traveled

I've traveled down
A long unwinding road
Uncertain of the future
So many obstacles in my way
The tears of rain surround me –
Perhaps a bird that is looking for his prey
Or is he really guiding me his way
A flower blooms – the trees resume
God gave us life –
Every breath we take –
Our journey is what
We choose to escape

Each day

Each day I wake
The pain consumes me –
It doesn't take long
The memories so fond
I close my eyes
And imagine you there –
Lying next to me –
Your warmth
Your embrace
Now –
The sun doesn't shine –
I hold you no longer –
My heart feels an ache
Like a sharp stabbing dagger

Future

The future will come
Behind the hidden curtain
Our lives are so uncertain
Tomorrow you will live
The past into the wind –
Or is it just a dream
The present full of wisdom
For how long will it last
Just to realize
You're not coming back

Trust Not

Trust not
The lies that hide
Between the walls
The light is on
But on the other side
False confessions
True deceit
A broken heart
Cut so deep

Everything Falls

Everything falls away
Every step yields a stone
Nothing is promised
Dreams are delusions
Or just an everlasting fantasy
Deep inside my heart
Scattered pieces of a broken soul
As I cry a gallon of tears

Rainbow

Magical rainbow
In the sky –
How your colors
Catch my eyes

Like soft whispers
God is calling my name –
Bringing me peace
From the heavenly sky

And all who can see you
As your colors reach wide
Sorrows will vanish
From deep inside

My journey
Has been a hard one –
Each day
I fought
To be strong
I always had courage
To keep
Holding on –
My kindness
Infectious –
My smile –
A song
Remember my love
Will continue
Beyond
I now am
An angel –
Not far away –
Just
Behind You

I remember the times
Not long ago
We laughed
We shared it all –
Then like a storm
Just passing by
You ended it all
Many years vested and
Our stories told
I put in my trust
To find it
Was nothing but a ruse
No good reason left –
Hit me like a wall
Forever my heart broken
That says it all

I Came in the Door

I came in the door
And what did I have?
Diarrhea – Diarrhea
I ran to the john
Pulled my pants down
All over the floor
Diarrhea – Diarrhea
The stench was so bad
Oh how I hate
This stinky place
If only I had worn a dependable –
Perhaps it would save me
A mess in my pants

Life is a battle

Life is a battle
One day the waters are still
The next your swimming upstream
Nothing is set in stone
Jagged rocks along the way
Where is the beauty
Does it shine through?
Or is it lost
On a mountain so high
Birds in the sky
They travel far
The journey goes on
In all hearts and minds

Friend

Friends can be found
Any day like a song – but
No one is as special
Since you came along

God chooses wisely –
Whose paths intertwine
For he knows whose hearts
And souls are to find

Every moment we spend passing
In space and in mind –
Brings us ever closer
Cherished friend of mine

God Sends

God sends
The rain, the snow
All kinds of weather
He gave us life
So, we can
Forgive one another
He always stands
Near us
With his open arms
And heals the
Heartache that
Lies deep inside

I am Thankful

I am thankful for this day –
For family, friends and the love we share
Not gifts, nor drinks, nor fancy feasts –
But being here today

I am thankful for each breath I take –
Being alive to see what's next –
I am thankful for the good and bad –
Life's lessons are a gift

I am thankful for being understood –
In a world of mystery
But most of all –
I am thankful for Jesus today –
Without him we would
Not be here

Merry Christmas

Hatred

The world is full of hatred
Every day someone is killed
Innocent people standing
Then shot for no given reason
I write in honor of their remembrance
But running out of space
Who will be the next one
In this world of nothing but hate?
But then again they were someone
A friend, a mother, a father, a son or daughter
Now called home to a better place
At least in the arms of Jesus
They will find peace

Raven In
The hazy sky –
You are my messenger
As you fly by –
Your black
Wings of beauty
So shinny and bright
You always stay
Near me
Through morning
And night –
My beautiful
Raven – Protector
And friend –
Please come
Back tomorrow
To see me again

Pray for You

I pray for you my friend –
That God lifts you from
Every pain
Every hurt
Heals you
And forever is there calling your name –
I pray He heals your
Body and gives you
Strength to be strong
As He touches
You as you weep –
I pray He be beside you –
In all your days to come
And guide you through
Your toughest times –
For He will
Never leave you

I will not worry about tomorrow
But be glad for today –
The sun is brightly shining –
Upon my face to light my way

Though we often stumble
As we plod along each day
If we reach for God's hand
He will surely
Show the way –

And as we travel through
This life and your rainbows
Are bending high
Do not take for granted
The blessings that we have

I've traveled

I've traveled down
A long unwinding road –
Uncertain of the future
So many obstacles in my way –
The tears of rain surround me –
Perhaps a bird looking for his prey
Or is he really guiding me his way?
A flower blooms – the trees resume
God gave us life
Every breath we take –
Our journey is what
We choose to escape

I'm Done

I'm done
I put in my time
No one really gives a damn
I've had enough
I'm not having fun
I'm done with the people
Who use me then lie
I'm done with the tears
I'm done with the pain
I'm done trusting people
Who rip out my soul
I've learned my lesson
And I've learned your lies
You only want me
When it suits your time
I'm done thinking of you
I'm done wondering what I've done
Your just not worth it anymore
I'm done

Look Into My Eyes

Look into my eyes
Tell me what you see
Do you see hurt
Do you see fear
Or is it just
A broken dream

Look into my eyes
Can you see my soul
Can you see all my memories
Or have I just lost control

Look into my eyes
And you will see
A heart that is deeper than
The greatest sea –

Look into my eyes
There you will see everything
I hold inside
There you will see me

Lost

The flowers have lost their fragrance
The stars have lost their shine
Tonight, I sit in emptiness
Thinking of lost time
Every path that I have followed
Every mountain I have climbed –
Just leads me
Back to lost memories
That clog up my endless mind
Tears fill my eyes like
Ocean waves –
Rippling until I'm blind
I will put this day
Behind me –
For tomorrow is not long away

I thought I could sit here
Feel safe from the world
And honor my savior
With family and friends
Then anger from nowhere
Approached us that day
No warning, no reason
We were targets, such rage
The enemy is waiting
Blood stains on his hands
But God came and Took us –
Away from the pain

Memories past –
Like a moment in time –
Gone so fast –
Like a flash
Of a camera
Then total darkness –
The person you were
No longer in focus –
Gone forever –
But dancing
Inside my mind
Turning and spinning
Like a merry-go-round
Is it a dream
Or a nightmare
I see?

Pain

Let me
take this time
to drown into
a wet day
Slowly let me
crumble like a wall
so carelessly built
Let me
feel the pain
of what
I never knew
before

My Heart

My heart feels like
It ruptured
Into a million tiny pieces of red marbles
Floating around
Endlessly –
Clusters of tears
Surround me
In a sea of empathy
Is it betrayal
Or life itself
That brings me to feel this way?
Never the best
The clock keeps turning
The sun will rise
And I will just keep searching
Someday I will
Find a friend

What a fool
I was to believe
We were friends
When you only
Pretended for
So many years
Every conversation
Was it a lie?
You took advantage
I saw no disguise
A simple gift
Meant nothing at all –
Breaking my heart
As you laugh
At it all
Never a memory
To your
Pathetic eyes
Leaving me with
Deep imprinted
scars

Patriot's Day

On this patriot's day race
With the sun in my eyes
My life was taken
No chance to say goodbye
The tears and the fire
The blood and survivors
My savior took me
To a place
We desire

It was a day we gathered here –
Excited to hear music and cheer –
But then the sound was coming near –
The rain of metal flying
Through the air
Running scared
One by one –
Some in pairs
Others left dead
All in seconds out of nowhere
The ground stained red
Who is this demon
Full of hatred and rage –
Who took
Away our life today?
The sound of bullets
Began to end –
As we looked up –
God took our hand

Today

The beginning
Of a lifetime –
One step at
A time –
Changes along
The way –
The wind
Will come –
The rain
Will pour –
The clouds empower –
And then
The sun
Will shine
For it
Becomes
tomorrow

Sadness
Comes like
A ball of
Fire –
Heating your
Emotions
Is this hell?
Then tear drops come
One then tons
Putting out
The flames
Until the
Next thought comes
And then
Back to
The beginning

I saw an image
In the sky –
Blinding me
As I looked
Deep within
It's pattern –
No words to
Explain
Just so beautiful
A mystery –
I believe
It's an angel
So majestic
So powerful
Following
My footsteps
Into tomorrow

An unwanted guest
Came to visit
In my dreams
Like nothing happened
She acted
Like a queen
Please go away
Can't you see
You have destroyed
Everything that
Used to be
My heart can't mend
From the dagger
You bring
My mind is
Cluttered from the
Past-you see
The trust is buried
Like unfound treasure
Locked away
It's called
Betrayal

Nightmares Haunt

My waking hours
Laughing in my face –
Darkness hiding
Inside my pillow
Pounding through my head –
Memories lost –
Forever gone
But dancing in my mind –
Is it day
Or night?
I don't know
What is right –
Only my heart
Is forever
broken

Parkinson's Disease

It was only yesterday –
I knew where I belonged –
So many memories –
Dancing in
My mind –
Like a symphony
But the song never ends –
Then, who are
The people who stand up and cheer?
Only an illusion –
Is this a dream?
I once was a mother,
A wife
And a friend –
Now all I remember
Is that time being at hand
I want to go home
Where there is peace
And no harm –
Where Jesus
Is waiting to
Take my hand

Music dances
In my soul –
Each note
Attacking my heart
Like a crow –
Bringing emotions
That I cannot control
Each phrase
Is connected
To the tears
That flow –
And when
The song comes
To the end –
It repeats
All over again

Crystal white
Snow upon
The tree branches –
Sparkle like
Diamonds
In the sky
Chilly winds
blowing in
My face
Forming ice
Crystals
On my cheek
Winter has not
Left us
The blossoms are
Dead
The tulips are frozen
When will it end

Time passes
Like the wind –
No answers
Just a void –
Memories encased
In my mind
Waiting for
Tomorrow but
Everything is gone –
Being torn apart –
Like a knife in my heart
Do you ever think
Of how selfish
You could be?
Nothing cherished to you
Just a dream
Waking up everyday
Without a past
Or memory

The world is
Full of violence –
What happened
To the past?
Around the corner
Bullets fly
Innocence forgotten –
A thief is
On the run –
Stealing what
Is mine
No conscious
No integrity
All treasures
Gone forever
Afraid to travel anywhere –
The hours
Tick away
Your life can end
In tragedy
In any second of
The day

Today just a casual one
Sun shining in my face
Long hours from my study place
Look forward to escape

A walk down to my favorite bar
A drink or two
And dinner too

The music loud
The TV on
People having fun line dancing

Then terror arrives
Gunfire in the air
One by one
Keep falling –
Blood stains are everywhere

There is no tomorrow
But God took away our
Sorrow

How do I know I'm secure and safe
When this world is so full of violence and hate?

How do I trust my neighbor, my friend –
When anger takes over and peace can't be found?

How can I stop these feelings of fear
When fire and terror are so very near?

The best I can do is pray for today,
And hope that tomorrow will be a better day

In Memory of My Sweet Dog Crissy

White as snow
Soft as feathers –
You filled our lives
With joy
Your eyes would sparkle
Like tiny diamonds
As you laid
So peaceful
By our side –
But the time
Has come
You are tired
And God has
Called you to his journey

Geese

Calm peaceful waters
I rest my wings –
Sun shining down
On my colorful eyes
Beauty beyond
For years I have found
The ponds and
The parks
Where I reside –
Please don't remove me
And Tear
Me Apart –
God brought me
Here where
I belong

Violence

I can't keep up
With today's violence
Gun shots heard –
One by one –
Red stains
Everywhere
Blood means nothing –
Or a beating heart –
Life is taken
In a moments time
Anger inside
Like a demon
On fire –
Taking what's
Not meant to be theirs –
Crying –
In a world
Of silent tears

Editor's Choice Award

Presented to

Patricia Shaw

for Outstanding Achievement in Poetry

Presented By

The National Library of Poetry

1997

Cynthia Stevens
Senior Editor

Caroline Sullivan
Senior Editor

Made in the USA
Lexington, KY
23 September 2019